The Dunkirk Escape

by

Jim Eldridge

Illustrated by Dylan Gibson

To Lynne, my inspiration as always.

With special thanks to:

Jinny Bain
Bilal El-Bhaireien
Aoife McCafferty
Samair Rahman
Monta Powers Simpson
Giorgio Tison
Steven Junior Woods

First published in 2009 in Great Britain by
Barrington Stoke Ltd
18 Walker St, Edinburgh, EH3 7LP

www.barringtonstoke.co.uk

ISBN: 978-1-84299-694-2

Printed in Great Britain by Bell & Bain Ltd

Contents

Chapter 1
Trapped!

BOOM!

The bomb blew up. It shook the ground and covered Dave Jones with sand and small rocks. All around him on the beach, soldiers tried to get some shelter. The shelling from the German big guns inland had been going on for hours. Now German planes had joined in, dropping bombs on the soldiers and shooting at them.

There must be about half a million of us soldiers packed onto this beach, Dave was thinking. Most were British. Some were French and Belgian. They were part of the Force that had been sent to France to beat Hitler's German army. But the Germans had crushed them.

Some of the soldiers had been killed during the fighting. Others had been taken prisoner by the Germans. The rest had fled to this beach on the French coast at Dunkirk. They hoped that the Navy would come and take them off the beach and back to England.

Rat-a-tat-tat-tat-tat!

Dave dived for cover as the German plane came in low, its guns blazing. He crawled down the beach to the sea. He hoped the wooden break-waters would give him some cover.

All round him men were looking for somewhere to hide from the big guns and the German planes. Many others had already been killed.

Dave looked out to sea. The coast of England was just 25 miles away, across the English Channel. He was thinking about his wife, Ann, and his 16-year-old son, Tom. They lived in Dover on the Kent coast.

Would he ever see them again, or would he die here?

Chapter 2
Mum Says No

Ann and Tom Jones sat in the living room of their small house in Dover and heard the bad news on the radio.

"400,000 soldiers are trapped on the beach at Dunkirk in France. They are under heavy attack from German forces. The

Royal Air Force and the Navy are preparing

a rescue bid."

Ann Jones switched off the radio.

"I can't bear to hear any more!" she said.

She began to cry. "400,000 men trapped, and

your dad could be one of them!"

"They'll get them off, Mum," said Tom.

The door opened and Tom's uncle Bill came in.

"Have you heard the news?" he asked.

Tom nodded.

"They've asked for men who would be willing to take their boats across the Channel and try and get our soldiers off the French beach," said Uncle Bill. "I'm taking my boat."

Uncle Bill was a fisherman who worked a small fishing boat.

"I'm coming with you, Uncle Bill!" said Tom.

"No!" said Ann Jones.

"But, Mum ..." Tom began to say.

"It's too awful that your dad is there, and Bill is going! I don't want to lose all the men in my family!" said his mum.

"Your mum's right, Tom," said Bill. "We'll need you young men to carry on the fight against Hitler if this goes wrong."

Bill patted Tom on the arm and left. Tom felt sick. He wanted to go with his uncle and save his dad.

Ann Jones got up.

"I'm going to see Mrs Hunt," she said. "Her husband will be on that beach as well. We wives need to help each other."

Tom waited until his mum had left the house. Then he grabbed his coat and ran down to the docks. Uncle Bill was just untying his small fishing boat. He was getting ready to leave. Along the docks other boats were being made ready to go. There were boats of all sizes, big and small. Some had motors and some had sails. Even the Dover ferry was being made ready.

"Mum said I can go with you!" shouted Tom.

Uncle Bill looked puzzled.

"I don't know," he said.

"Let the boy come," said Ned.

Ned was an old sailor who worked with Uncle Bill on the boat.

"I started at sea when I was just twelve years old," said Ned. "And it's Tom's dad that's stuck on that beach."

"OK, Tom," said Uncle Bill. "You can come."

Tom jumped on board. Bill revved up the engine, and the small boat set off from the docks. As the boat moved into the open waters of the English Channel, Tom felt sick. It wasn't the rocking of the boat on the waves – he was used to that. He felt sick because he knew that he was going to war!

Chapter 3
Bomb

Dave Jones hid in the sand dunes. Thousands of other soldiers were with him in the dunes. They had dug holes for themselves in the sand with their bare hands. The sand gave some shelter from the bullets that rained down on them from the German fighter planes.

The air was filled with smoke from
bombs and fires. But up on the sand dunes
Dave had a good view of the sea. He could
see past the smoke right along the beach to
the port of Dunkirk. It was about a mile
away. Thick black smoke rose above the
town. Fires were still burning. The

Germans had bombed the port to stop any ships from coming in or out.

There was a wooden jetty sticking out into the sea from the beach. Some soldiers were hiding under the jetty, in the water.

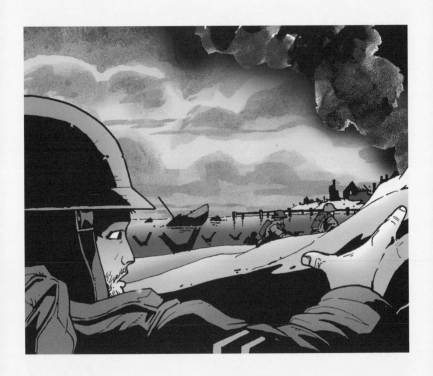

They were hoping a boat would come to the jetty and they could escape.

The soldier lying in the sand next to Dave said, "We'll never get off this beach."

"Yes, we will," said Dave. "The Royal Navy will send ships to get us off."

The other soldier laughed.

"I've been on this beach for three days, mate," he said. "The Royal Navy has tried sending in ships. Most of them have got sunk. Look out to sea. You can see bits of the sunken ships sticking out of the water. Look!"

Dave looked. The other soldier was right. About a mile out to sea Dave saw things poking out of the water. At first he took them to be naval defences put in the sea by the Germans against an attack. Now he saw they were the tips of boat funnels and other broken bits of metal.

Then he saw something else beyond the smoke. A Royal Navy ship had put down its anchor about a mile off the beach, and a small boat had been let down into the water and was heading away from it towards the wooden jetty.

"There's a boat coming!" shouted Dave. He was very excited.

He got up, ready to run down the beach to the jetty.

"Don't bother," said the other soldier. "You'll never get on it. There are loads of men waiting at the jetty."

"I don't care!" said Dave. "I want to get back home!"

Dave ran down the slope of sand to the jetty. The small boat had just got there and already men were climbing into it.

"Wait for me!" yelled Dave.

A noise made him look up. In the sky above him there was a German bomber. A large shape dropped from the plane. It was a bomb. It was dropped down right onto the jetty.

"Look out!" shouted Dave.

But it was no use. His shout couldn't be heard above the noise.

The bomb hit the small boat and the jetty. There was a huge bang and the air was filled with fire and smoke and the sound of screams.

When the smoke cleared, the jetty and the small boat had vanished. All that was left was bits of burning wood and bodies.

Someone was standing beside Dave. It was the other soldier.

"See?" said the soldier. "What did I say? We'll never get off this beach!"

Chapter 4
The Destroyer

Uncle Bill's small fishing boat went up and down with the waves. Ned was at the wheel, keeping the boat on course for France. Tom and Bill were at the bow of the small boat. All round them hundreds of other small boats were bobbing about on the water, all heading towards the French coast.

They tried to keep well away from each other. In front of them huge black clouds hung over the port of Dunkirk.

"The Germans have set the town on fire," said Bill.

Tom could see the planes in the sky over the French coast. There were small fighter planes, and also larger bombers.

Bill pointed at the water all round the boat. It was black with oil.

"It looks like they've sunk lots of ships as well."

Far off they could hear the sound of big guns being fired.

"Those are the guns of German tanks you can hear," said Bill. "They've got our lads trapped."

As they got closer to the French coast, Tom could see the remains of ships. Here and there part of a funnel poked out of the water. As Bill had said, the German bomber planes had sunk many British Navy ships.

They passed by a Royal Navy destroyer about half a mile off-shore. The small boats bringing soldiers from the beach were pulling up along-side the destroyer and off-loading them. The destroyer was giving the small boats cover by firing its guns at the attacking German planes.

"That's what we'll do," said Bill. "We'll pick men off the beach and take them to that destroyer. That way we can rescue a lot more than if we tried to take them all the way back to England."

"And we won't have to face my angry mum," said Tom to himself. Tom knew that as soon as they got back to England his mum would order him off the boat, and Bill would have to agree. But Tom was going to find his dad first and bring him back home.

Chapter 5
Under Attack

As Ned steered the small fishing boat into the shallow water near the beach, Tom's heart sank. There were thousands and thousands of men, all dressed in the same brown uniforms. There was no way he would be able to spot his dad in among all these men.

It was awful. There were dead bodies of soldiers in the water. Some were face down. Was one of them his dad?

"I can't see Dad," Tom said.

"We'll have to help those we can," said Bill. "With a bit of luck, your dad will be picked up by someone else if we don't find him."

"But we came here to save Dad!" said Tom.

Bill shook his head.

"We came here to save as many as we could," he said. "I hope one of them's your dad."

Ned slowed the engine of the boat and they drifted in nearer the shore. Men were waiting for them up to their necks in water.

"Stop here!" shouted Bill to Ned. "If we get stuck on a sand-bank we'll never get off!"

Ned put the engine of the boat into idle. Bill and Tom reached down and helped the men in the water clamber up the ropes and

nets that hung down the side. The boat
began to sink lower in the water as more
men climbed on board.

"No more!" shouted Bill to the waiting
soldiers.

Some of the waiting men tried to climb on board, but Bill pushed them back into the water.

"If we take you now we could sink!" he shouted. "We'll come back for you!"

Ned reversed the boat out into deeper water, and then turned and headed for the destroyer that was waiting off-shore. Other small boats were doing the same, all floating low in the water because there were so many soldiers on board.

As they got near the destroyer, Tom heard the sound of a plane getting near. He looked up. It was a German fighter plane.

"Everyone get down!" shouted Bill.

Everyone ducked down on the deck.
There was the sound of the plane's machine
guns firing, and bits of wood flew off the
boat as the bullets hit it. The glass of the
wheel-house was smashed, and Tom saw
blood on Ned's face. Ned had been hit!

Tom got up and went to go to the wheel-house to take over the wheel, but Ned waved him back.

"It's only glass cuts!" shouted Ned.

The destroyer began firing at the German plane, and there was the sound of an explosion over-head as the destroyer's guns hit their target. Tom saw the German fighter plane on fire, thick black smoke pouring from it as it fell out of the sky and crashed into the sea.

Chapter 6
Still Looking

Time passed. Tom was feeling worn out. The clothes and faces of Tom, Bill and Ned were black with smoke from the fires that burned on the beach and with oil from the sea.

They'd gone to and fro between the French beach and the destroyers anchored out in deeper water about 20 times. On each trip they'd brought 30 men off the beach. But none of them had been his dad. Each time they'd set back towards the coast Tom had hoped that this would be the time he'd find his dad, but each time they came back to the destroyer with 30 strangers on board.

Was his dad still alive?

Chapter 7
Going Home

Dave Jones stood up to his knees in the sea water. Day-light was fading. The firing from the German tanks had stopped for the moment. The German bombers and fighter planes were still overhead, but they were firing at the boats and not at the soldiers on the beach. In spite of the German planes, the small boats kept on coming. They'd already taken off thousands of men, but there were still thousands more trapped on the beaches.

Dave moved forward into deeper water.

"I must get on a boat!" he said to himself. "I must see Ann and Tom again before I die!"

He pushed against the waves. The water was up to his chest now. His sopping wet uniform dragged him down, but he struggled on, walking out, aiming for the boats.

Other soldiers were doing the same, and Dave found himself pressed against others

in the crush. He walked on. By now the
water was up to his chin.

"If this water gets any deeper I'm going
to drown!" he said to himself.

He stepped forward, and suddenly the
ground fell away. He sank under the water.

He felt a boot step on his back, and a feeling of panic came over him. He was going to be trodden under foot by the other men!

In panic Dave grabbed at legs near him, and dragged himself back up. As his head came up above the water, he opened his mouth and took a great gulp of fresh air. Then he heard a voice shout out, "Dad!"

It sounded like his son, Tom.

"I must be dreaming!" Dave said. "Tom's in England."

Then he felt hands grab him and drag him out of the water and onto the deck of a small fishing boat. It was a boat that he

knew well. It was his brother Bill's boat.

Other men fell onto the deck beside him, and then he felt the boat reversing away from the shore, and turning out to sea.

Dave looked into the faces of the two men who'd pulled him on board. They were black with smoke but he knew who they were. One was Bill. The other was Tom!

Tom grinned at his dad.

"We've got you, Dad!" he said. "We're going home."

The Real History

Early in the Second World War, in May 1940, nearly 400,000 Allied troops, most of them British, had been forced to retreat to the French coast at Dunkirk by the Germans. A fleet of British, French and Belgian naval ships set off to try and get the trapped soldiers off the beaches. But these ships were shelled by German guns on the shore and bombed by German planes from the air.

There were also torpedo attacks by U-boats.

Between 29 May and 4 June 1940, a fleet of 900 fishing boats, small sailing boats and the like set sail across the Channel to join the Royal Navy ships. They belonged to ordinary people who just wanted to help. These small boats and the navy ships took 340,000 troops safely off the beaches at Dunkirk and back to England.

Lucky

by
S. P. Gates

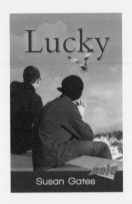

Everyone thinks that because Dom is big, he's a bully. But his best friend Leon knows what he's really like. And when an injured gull needs their help, Leon finds out there's even more to Dom.

You can order *Lucky* from our website at
www.barringtonstoke.co.uk

The Night Runner

by
Alan Combes

Greg wants to win the race. Every night
he trains in secret on the school field. But
he sees a spooky shape in the moon-light.
What is it? Should he run for his life?

You can order *The Night Runner* from our website at
www.barringtonstoke.co.uk

Flash Flood

by
Andy Croft

Jaz and Toni are trapped and the water is
rising ... Can they make it
out in time?

You can order *Flash Flood* from our website at
www.barringtonstoke.co.uk

Cliff Edge

by
Jane A. C. West

Can Danny make the climb of his life to save his friend? No ropes, no help – no hope?

You can order *Cliff Edge* from our website at www.barringtonstoke.co.uk